FROM

VICTIM

TO

VIRTUOUS

for

LITTLE GIRLS

FROM

VICTIM

TO

VIRTUOUS

for

LITTLE GIRLS

JUST BECAUSE I AM LITTLE DOES NOT MEAN THAT I AM NOT HURTING...

DOES ANYONE HEAR MY CRY?

YOLANDA MARSHALL

CONTENT

SPECIAL THANKS

God, I ask that you continue pouring into my life what you want me to pour into the lives of others through my written work. I want to thank all those who support me in my endeavors. May God continue blessing each of you!

What is the definition of the following words? You will see these words throughout the book.

Victim — a person who is hurt by another.

Virtue — behavior showing high moral standards.

Virtuous --pure, righteous, morally excellence.

Brokenness — separated into parts or pieces, shattered.

Wholeness — the concept that we contain all potentials -- potentials for any action, thought, or energy tone (e.g., emotion or feeling).

Conditions — the state of something.

Characteristics — the quality of a person.

Consequences — something that happens as a result of a particular action.

Worth — the value or something or someone.

Transition — a change from one thing to the next.

Simulating — to imitate

Environment — condition by which one is surrounded.

Source: Used the Merriam-Webster and other dictionary references online via Google search to define these words and other words used throughout this book.

FROM VICTIM TO VIRTUOUS

Many of you are victims of common conditions in your lives. Some of you may have been neglected in the home, at school, at church, and even in your community, and this has caused some of you to make bad decisions, even at such a young age. You may be a victim of brokenness (I explain what I mean by brokenness in Chapter 1—read on).

I was once a victim of brokenness, which had a negative impact on my life— but God, delivered me! It is my desire that upon reading *From Victim to Virtuous for Little Girls*, you will claim and receive the position God has intended for you to become—A Virtuous, Little Girl.

THE VIRTUOUS LITTLE GIRL…

A virtuous, little girl is vigilant. She is important, righteous, truthful, understanding, obedient, and an overcomer. She is talented, extraordinary, energetic, nice, good, influential, royal, and likable.

Yolanda Marshall

I want each of you to understand that you will grow into a virtuous woman of God. Look at what the Word of God says about a virtuous woman (read it with your mother or guardian):

THEWord of God says: "Who can find a virtuous woman for her price is far above rubies. The heart of her husband doth safely trust in her, so that he shall have no need of spoil. She will do him good and not evil all the days of her life. She seeketh wool, and flax, and worketh willingly with her hands. She is like the merchants ship; she bringeth her food from afar. She riseth also while it is yet night, and giveth meat to her household and a portion to her maidens. She considereth a field, and buyeth it; with the fruit of her hands. She planteth a vineyard. She girdeth her loins, with strength, and stregtheneth her arms.

She perceiveth that her merchandise is good. Her candle goeth not out by night. She layeth her hands to the

11

spindle, and her hands hold the distaff. She stretcheth out her hand to the poor; yea, she reacheth forth her hands to the needy, she is not afraid of the snow for her household, for all her household are clothed with scarlet. She maketh herself coverings of tapestry; her clothing is silk and purple. Her husband is known in the gates, when he sitteth among the elders of the land. She maketh fine linen and selleth it; and delivereth girdles unto the merchant. Strength and honour are her clothing; and she shall rejoice in time to come.

She openeth her mouth with wisdom; and in her tongue is the law of kindness. She looketh well to the ways of her household, and eateth not the bread of idleness. Her children arise up, and call her blessed; her husband also, and he praiseth her. Many daughters have done virtuously, but thou excellest them all. Favour is deceitful, and beauty is vain; but a woman that feareth the Lord, she shall be praised. Give her of the fruit of her hands; and let her own works praise her in the gates."

Proverbs 31:10-31

INTRODUCTION

O NE of the most blessed gifts of all is that you as a girl claim a young Girl's status. This separates you from any other name that is given...that is to say *A VIRTUOUS, LITTLE GIRL*. I want to help you understand what I mean by "any other name that is given..." Oftentimes boys and men will call girls and women bad names; it is common to hear this in some rap music, and some of you may even hear boys' call girls bad names at school, in your community, etc. This is not to say that all boys call girls bad names, but there are a lot of them who do. What I want you to always focus on in life is being called a good name. In Proverbs 22:1 we read, "A good name is rather to be chosen than great riches, and loving favour rather than silver and gold."

All girls were born with the seed of virtue. When the seed is nourished (provide with what is needed in life) and watered daily, it allows each of you to grow into great teen girls, and then women of valor (worth). A girl of virtue positively affects everyone in her world from her household to her school, from even strangers she might come in contact with in passing.

Now before you read on I would like to offer this prayer: *Lord, help these little girls to love, surrender, and see themselves through your eyes — based on love not judgment. Allow them to see each other as being made in your image. Father, help them all to fear less and love more. Allow them to pray for each other and not talk about each other. Help them to see that the bad behavior that some of them may have experienced so young could possibly be based upon something that happened to cause them to become broken. Let them not look down on their peers because some of them have dark skin or light skin, have brown skin or white skin, tall or short, thin or overweight. Lord, these little girls are becoming more like you — virtuous. Unforgiveness, jealously, hate, envy, fear, poor self-image, and other doubts must be eliminated while they are little girls. They will not glorify any woman, man, or child — only You deserve all the glory. Amen.*

I have written this book to share with little girls all across the globe. All of you can possess the characteristics of a virtuous girl and grow into virtuous women and become your best self in life. God sees where you are now, and knows your end.

My prayer is that this book will help shed light on the dark areas of your life, and help you to find yourself in light of who you can be and have been purposed to be. The path to truth and deliverance to gain freedom is for everyone. If you are broken, I am certain that this book will help guide you in a direction of becoming that whole, virtuous, little girl. So many of us virtuous women can identify with the challenges that life has presented to us, even when we were children, and we can encourage you while you are still a little girl. If you would be open and share how you feel with your mother, aunt, or some other positive figure in your life, you can become stronger as a child and defeat the enemy (the Devil) on every hand.

Note: My story is shared in three parts. You may have your mother (or guardian) to read each part with you to help you identify with some of the content that you may not fully understand as a little girl. This three part story has to be shared before you proceed with the chapters in order to help you on your journey in life. Part two will serve as a reminder for you as you grow — not to take the direction that I took to gain love, attention and affection (feeling, liking) from the opposite sex. There are Bible Scripture references in this book that your mother (or guardian) can read with you and help you understand, too. They can also help to answer some other questions that you may have as you read each chapter. As you and your mother read my story together, I pray that you two bond even closer.

PART ONE

MY journey in essence does not start with me. My journey starts with my mother who realized that she was the product of a journey before she was my mother. I always knew there was something special about my mother. Well, actually, there are 12 others who also call her mother. She was definitely being fruitful. My mother would be the first to rise in the morning and the last to lie down at night. She was prayerful, generous and sensitive. She truly had the gift of virtue. She was a virtuous woman, BUT...

I can never do justice to my mother's virtue—well, the dynamics of my mother's virtue—without saying my dad. Her husband! Yes, he was! He died in 1997, but my memory of him is long lasting. He was tall and handsome, with those gray eyes. A good man he was, yet he was also abusive, fussy, angry...and most of all he was controlling. He was full of energy and laughter. I loved my dad! He loved his children, too. But he had a strange way of showing his love. He was a provider, yet we were living in poverty. We will take a deeper look at this later.

I now realize my mother was a symbol of virtue, but she was broken. She was very strong, yet weakened by brokenness. This was the foundation by which life began to build the person that I am today. To understand who I am today, we have to open the Pandora's Box of the journey called: *My Life*.

When I was a little girl, I would get on my knees every night and pray, *"Thou lay me down to sleep; I pray to the Lord my soul to keep, if I should die before I wake, I pray to the Lord my soul to take."* As a child, I took that prayer very seriously because I really did not think I was going to wake up after having those bad dreams of my mother being beaten by my father, and those giant rats crawling in our bedroom. I could barely go to sleep—all I heard was his loud voice calling my mother everything, but a child of God—you…you…you. I could not tell which one was worse—his loud voice or the rats squeaking throughout the night. My father even called us, the children, bad names, too.

Every morning I was awakened by the smell of my mother's good ole southern breakfast. Biscuits, eggs, and bacon were my favorite breakfast food items. When I opened my eyes, the first things I saw were feet…right by my mouth—the feet of one of my sisters. There were three of us to one bed. The bedroom was small. Two beds could barely fit in the room. We had one dresser for our clothing, which obviously was not enough space for the tees, panties and socks of six little girls (and two more to come later). Everything that could not fit in the drawers was stored in garbage bags and placed in the closet.

We had to rise very early each morning because there was only one bathroom for the girls and boys. We had to make it quick when it was our turn because there were so many of us. While exiting the bathroom, I could hear the voice of my sister, "Landa, what are you going to wear today?" I answered, "I don't know." Then, I would go through the bags and pull out something that had already been worn by one of my sisters the day before.

After everyone got dressed, prayed over our food, and ate, we would yell, "See you later, Mom and Dad! We'll see y'all this evening!" Out the door we went. As we were on our way to school, I could not help but think about what my mom had told us about our behavior and making good grades. She was serious about each of her children earning an education. She did not play about slacking in our school work. We all knew you had better not bring a bad grade home or that was your butt!

My mother made sure we did our homework when we arrived home each evening. Oftentimes she would pop up at the school. You had to be on your best behavior all the time because you did not know when she would show up unannounced. We were expected to make good grades on our schoolwork and have the best behavior while at school. Good grades and bad behavior were not tolerated. Even with all of her encouragement, some of us still slacked in making good grades, and being on our best behavior. But I could not just think about my mom's expectations of our making good grades. In addition, I thought about the shame that I was about to face from classmates that recognized I was wearing the same outfit my sister wore the day before. It was typical for the sisters to wear each other's clothes. Oh, do not mention other things they decided to find wrong with me...my hair, my shoes, my looks...so it was rather hard to focus on making good grades when I really did not want to be there. I knew that I was going to face this issue everyday until something changed.

And looking through a child's eye, I did not see our situation getting any better. Poverty (poor, not having much) seemed to have overtaken us, and not only poverty. Unfortunately, I did not see my mother or father getting dressed for work each morning. "How are things going to get better?" I asked. Well, now I can see why my mom could not work a 9-to-5 job. Her full-time job was to raise her children. My father's monthly veteran's check was the only income, and it barely provided our needs.

Now wearing each other's clothes was not the only

typical thing. It was also common for me to wear a face of hurt and awe. This was all because of the restless, unpeaceful, and unforgettable nights. Strange things would happen between sunset and sunrise. To tell someone the truth about this situation, often means that the innocent are told something in response, which can make you feel like everything and anything, but a child of God. And you are often called a liar and made to feel that if something did happen—which they do not believe happened—it is all your fault. The innocent are often made to suffer for peace sake.

The older I became, the worse I felt. I knew that I was going to face so many familiar faces that did not quite understand the true essence of my position—how I was living—how I was violated—and how this affected me.

As stated before, my father only received a government check that was not enough to get us out of poverty. I remember my father doing handy work every now and again, a couple of times a month—maybe three or more. I heard he had his own heating business, but that was before my time. I am not certain what happened to my father's business. But my father had the strangest kind of hustle, and he involved his children. He said that he knew of a way to earn extra money. After he shared it with us, I thought his idea was really scary.

I had just started high school, and I wanted to enjoy my teenage years. The weekends were the only time I could think about having fun because mom wanted us to focus on our school work during the week. While I was thinking about having the teenage fun on the weekends, not run the streets but have that freedom to enjoy my sisters, brothers, and our close friends — my father had another plan in mind.

This was the earning "extra money" plan. He would order huge amounts of donuts for us to sell in the strangest, yet dangerous places — the liquor stores. As I looked at this picture through a child's eye, I knew something was not right. My siblings also knew something was wrong with this! If we ever asked him the question, "Why do we have to go to the liquor stores to sell donuts?" He would cuss us out completely. With that in mind, we had no option. Well, I guess we did have options. And that was choosing which liquor store we wanted to stand in front of to sell donuts. We were taught to be obedient. But this time it was very hard to submit to his rules.

We would gather around the room and talk about who would pair up for which liquor store. "Which one do you want to go to?" I asked my sister. Hurry up! The decision needs to be made quickly because you know Mom and

Dad will be back in a few minutes, and he is going to be ready to load up.

Sure enough, when Dad arrived with the trunk filled with donuts, you better have been ready to load up or that was your butt. He would get out of the car and come in the house, "Are y'all ready?" He asked. Well, if we were not ready, he would just put us into pairs. One of my sisters and I were standing in the front room when he said, "I'm taking y'all to Avondale liquor store." He told the other siblings, "Your mom and I will be back to pick y'all up. There's not enough room in the car."

It only took us about 10 minutes to get to our destination. The frowns on our faces did not last long. Once we arrived, we drove to the side of the building, started unloading the donuts, and positioned ourselves on the small brick attached to the building that could barely hold us up. "Smile," "Smile," he would say as he drove off. "I'll be back to pick y'all up in a couple of hours. But if y'all finish before I get back, just call me." I felt as though my own father was using us. If you are thinking what my mom had to say about all of this, well, sometimes she also had to go with us.

I can remember the disappointing look on my sister's face. We were both unhappy. It was very embarrassing because we always saw someone we knew each time we had to go. Even worse, some of our classmates would show up with their relatives. We felt as though we were so alone. We thought to ourselves: "What can we do?" We can't run...we can't dodge...and we can't even hide.

The shame we felt when we had to dodge the children we went to school with, and those in the neighborhoods, were fresh on our minds. It was as fresh as the donuts. The only difference is the shame lasted longer than the boxes of donuts we were selling. Each Monday, I could only pray that I would not be criticized at school.

After this so-called hustle was being repeated every weekend, the question was asked to my mother this time. "Why do we have to go to the liquor stores to sell donuts?" She replied, "I have to go, too! That's your dad who's got y'all out there." We had to ask her everything in secret because my dad was so controlling.

The sad part of this hustle was lying about the church. Yes, my dad told us to lie about the church! We had to tell the customers we were selling donuts for our church. Actually, I was not a member of a church at the time, but some of my siblings were. The question was asked, "Why lie about the church?" He said, "They would not know. Most of those customers may not ask anyway. Their minds are on drinking that whiskey." Well, sure enough, one Sunday morning my sister's pastor announced that someone had been standing in front of liquor stores lying about the church. Oh, what an embarrassment it was—somebody must have told!

Yeah, speaking of my dad's response to the customer's having their minds on drinking that whiskey…One day, my sister and I were standing in front of the liquor store, and we approached an angry male customer and asked, "Hi, Mr. Would you like to buy a box of donuts or give a donation to our church?" He said, "No. I don't want to buy any (blank) donuts." Well, he was full of whiskey and he was going to buy more. I wish you could have seen the look on his face when my sister asked him if he wanted to buy some donuts. He just started attacking her. I was so scared. I did not know what to do. I was only 14 years old. My sister started crying and I panicked.

She told me to run across the street to the store to call my dad. I wanted so badly for her to go with me, but she did not want to leave the donuts in front of the store. I called my dad to tell him what happened. He was so angry with us. He said, "I just dropped y'all (blank) off." I said, "But this man is attacking her." Sadly, he did not arrive until much later when it was close for the store to close.

The seeds of frustration, agitation, confusion, anger and resentment were planted within me. Some of my siblings also felt this way. After seeing the physical and mental abuse of my mother and siblings, it was hard for me to receive my father. Although I still loved him, I was so ready to move from under his roof. When I started my junior year in high school, I started counting down the days that remained under this roof. This was also the year I turned 16 years old, so I was permitted to date.

PART TWO

I want to talk about those bad relationships that I had submitted (yield) to, and two of those relationships led to decisions that resulted in me bringing two children into this world —all due to my brokenness. I also want to talk about how those relationships distracted me from focusing on what God had intended for me and how they played a big part in my going down paths that blocked my spiritual, emotional, social, financial, and mental growth. One of the most important things to give attention to in this matter, as stated before, is that I was 16 years old when I was told that I could date (talk to boys).

From my first relationship, the first guy I dated (the one who I had my firstborn child with) up to the second marriage and divorce at the age of 31, I had been in transition. I went from man to man. I went into these relationships looking through the eyes of my parents. That is to say, the only things they seemed to have been able to see and value was money and material provisions. Never mind the emotional, spiritual, mental sensitivity, and provision was all about what I have come to call the "M and M" provision, *"Money and Material."*

I found myself accepting any type of behavior simply

because I was looking for just one thing in a man (M and M), and I thought it was the right thing to do. But once I submitted to such behavior, everything that was hidden on the inside of him started to show its face during the relationship. It is what hindered me and kept me going backwards year after year, one relationship at a time. This happened because I allowed myself to become emotionally attached each time I entered a new relationship. I was a person who struggled with low self-esteem for many years, so it was not easy to walk away each time, no matter how bad the relationship was.

I was 17 years young, confused, and broken when I had my first child. I did not know anything about mothering a child because I was still a child myself. I was a senior in high school, trying to take care of a baby that I did not have full knowledge of how to nurture, other than change the diaper and feed her a bottle when she would cry. I also cannot forget that I did have to get up with her throughout the night. My mother and father enforced this because they said I had made my bed hard, so I had to lay in it. They would so often say this.

I was not financially able to take care of a child. The welfare system was all I knew, just like so many of the young girls and ladies I saw as I was growing up. I applied for welfare and food stamps so that I could provide for my daughter. I was amazed that I could only receive $137 per month in welfare. Clearly, this was not enough to take care of a child. Besides, I was nearly grown, and my parents could barely support me; and they certainly could not afford to feed another mouth and all of the other necessary obligations.

My child was my full responsibility. I had made an adult's decision with a child's mind. Because of this decision, my parents were forced to play the mother and father role in my absence, while I attended high school. Although I had not graduated from high school, I had the responsibilities of a mother when I came home each day from school. There was no mistake about this! I had to act the role that I created for myself as a mother. The consequences of my decision immediately came into play. I will never forget those restless nights as a high school student having to take on this kind of adult responsibility. *Can you imagine how that could have felt?* I know that you are just a little girl, but have you ever tried staying awake in the late hour on the weekend watching TV? I am certain that you were really tired, right? Well, I had to stay up every night to feed my baby, rock her to sleep, and then rise very early to go to school the next morning. This is my story! I don't want this to be your story. This is what happened as a result of a bad choice that I made.

I can even remember having to catch that big, yellow school bus every morning, right across from Whatley Elementary School. There were six or more of us waiting for the bus to arrive around 7:15 a.m. I stayed to myself as we stood there waiting for the bus to arrive. Each of us who waited for the bus was from different backgrounds, but we had so much in common. We were all very young, and each of us carried a child that we could not possibly take care of at such a young age. I was not perfect and I had not mastered my mothering skills, but it was apparent that the majority of the other young mothers also had no clue.

As we would load the bus, often I would think about and ask myself, *"Why are so many young girls even having babies?"* I now understand and I have some of the answers. Could it be a cycle? Did the mother have her first baby at a young age? Could it be because of peer pressure? Could it be because of what is shown on the television? Could it be because of what is heard on the radio? I will have to say "Yes!" to each of these questions.

I had many thoughts of dropping out of school because I did not have any parenting skills I needed. Although I have always had a mothering spirit (that does make a difference), yet I was new to the mothering experience. I still had to learn how to become a mother. It is fair to say that my parents and others always recognized me as a nurturer, even when I was very young. My dad would always say, "There's something special about Landa. She has a good heart."

I always wanted to help people. I was always in the kitchen helping my mother prepare meals for the entire family. I also helped take care of my younger siblings. As I look back, dedication, patience, wisdom, and unconditional mother's love is definitely what was, and still is, required to raise children. The wisdom of God has taught me how to become the mother I have been purposed to be, in spite of the fact that I had my first child at a young age.

My pregnancy was embarrassing. I knew so many girls my age, those who I walked to school with, who were focused on their education and going to college. Because of my pregnancy, I did not have a clear view of going to college. I did not realize how it could have impacted my life positively. But I am thankful for my sister, Cathy, who encouraged me to finish high school because there were only a few months remaining before graduation. Believe me! I really needed encouragement during this time in my life.

My first child was born three months before my high school graduation. I graduated in 1991. All of my hope of going to college had totally faded. I did not want to leave my baby to go to college. Although I still maintained the value of education, which my mother had instilled in me and my siblings, the decision to delay attending college was one of my circumstances. My hope and focus was to be there for my baby until she was older.

Do you remember me telling you about how I was ready to get out from under my father's roof? Well, the time had come. I was just turning 18 years old, when my child's father and I moved in together. We moved into this community which appeared to be safe, but later realized that we were surrounded by several people who had drug habits; it seemed like these people did not go to sleep.

Now moving in with a man was definitely something new for me. If there was one thing I remember always being told besides you need a provider, it was that you do not need to shack up with a man. Now those two things I had heard clearly. I had heard this advice ever since I could remember. Yet, this new place in my life offered something my parents repeatedly expressed: Provision. This, I will always remember. The decision for me to live with my child's father was a high-impact decision that has had an impact on my life in ways that only in recent years I have been blessed to truly understand.

This was a tough decision for me, but at that time I was just ready to move. And I thought my child's father could offer me M and M (*money and material*) as he proved to do as a young qualified provider. Yet, there was more. I did not quite know all that love was supposed to be. The kind of love that my father had shown all my life was both hurtful at times, and confusing. What I did know is that I, as well as my daughter, needed the love of a man who was not angry, verbally abusive, or would mentally drain me. However, what I failed to realize is that the hurting child on the inside of me had not yet been healed.

I experienced real love all right. As time progressed, it seems as though I was reliving my childhood experience of love as I had done under my father's roof. Now this was a different roof, but things seemed so familiar. Just as I had seen my father hustle to make a living and "provide" by having us sell donuts in front of liquor stores, placing us in harm's way, this was a new representation of a conflicting past which had placed all of my siblings in danger. Yes, it was quite dangerous. Well, with my child's father, I was forced to be involved in a different kind of hustle {drug dealing}—a different kind of danger.

The danger of this hustle came into play soon after it started. One night I found myself fighting to go to sleep as my child's father left to work the overnight shift, leaving my daughter and me alone with his cousin to carry out his hustle. As I tossed and turned, I found myself lying on my left side, and I could see his cousin entering my dark bedroom, as the reflection of the moonlight shined through my window, making it obvious for me to capture the view of a gun being held to his back by another man. Yes, he was being robbed — everything he had, to what was stored in our bedroom had been taken. Now here I am pretending to be asleep, yet shaking and praying that God will deliver me from this unsafe environment.

This incident was followed by another time when a stranger hid behind our kitchen wall waiting with his gun for the first person breathing to come home — he was in motion to rob us. The very next day, my child's father was upset I did not come home the night this occurred (I felt a deep yearning within to stay away on this night). He expressed that this man indeed tried to rob him and there was a great struggle between the two of them, both firing their guns as the stranger fled the scene.

This was the kind of hustle that required me to dodge when necessary, find a hiding place, and sleep with one eye open. Speaking of sleeping with one eye open, it was true that I could only sleep with one eye open for at least a week because I could not open my left eye. My child's father had kicked me in my left eye with his steel-toed boots that he was wearing on the night of this fighting match. This happened shortly after we split up. I guess that was better than having my brains blown out with a nine-millimeter Glock (a gun) that he held between my eyes threatening to kill me, then himself. He was doing this because I had found interest in somebody else who I thought could love me better, trying to escape all this madness of the sleepless nights, uninvited strangers — the robbers, addictive customers…it was not the best way to escape, nonetheless, it was time.

Let me say this — facing a gun was not anything new for me. The first person who pulled a gun on me was my father. He pulled a rifle on me. One day, I went over to visit my parents, only to find them in a heated argument — this was not new either. The argument stemmed from my father's decision to give one of my brothers' girlfriend money to get her hair fixed, instead of one of my sisters. I know you are probably thinking, *her brother's girlfriend*? Yes, he divided the brothers and sisters when we were children; even now the spirit of division exists within our family. My father would imply, *my sons will always carry my name, and my daughters will carry somebody else's name.* In essence, he was saying that he would take care of my brothers' girlfriends/wives before he would take care of his own daughters. This was really silly; it was stated numerous times. Now on the day this madness occurred, at least half of us were all grown up and dating. But on this particular day, the verbal abuse, which consisted of bad name calling (a female dog), was not done just in front of family anymore. It was done in the presence of one of my brothers' girlfriend.

But my mother had now gained some energy (she spoke a peace of her mind) to defend her children after many years of our family being abused, namely her daughters. Not only did my mother gain energy to defend her children, I found myself defending my mother this day by standing up for what was right. Well, as I stood up for what was right, I was wronged by having to dodge a bullet as I drove my red Nissan Sentra off the curb in fear of being shot by my father, coupled with risking being hit by a car head on because I was watching the gun instead of the street. Now I was facing two endangerments at the same time. I was not the only one in danger; one of my younger sisters was in the car with me.

What another sad image to identify with love! "Was this love?" This is the question I had been asking seemingly all my life. I was ready to experience this thing called real, love. I found out it was not in material things because my child's father gave me all of that. It was not in the money. I had a substantial amount of that, too. I had been cussed out, fussed at, had a gun pulled on me, and called bad names by my father, so I knew it could not have been in that. But the question was asked, "How can someone love you—unconditionally, if they don't love themselves?"

I had dated this "provider" for more than five years. He was definitely my high school sweetheart. After he had created an environment obviously not safe for my child and me, with all the chaos, confusion, and abuse—I knew it was time for me to move on.

So, I met a friend who I thought could love me better. Yes, this was the man I had met toward the end of my first relationship. I did not even think about recovery. We started a relationship that lasted for about a year. There I was, in transition. As we were approaching a year of dating, he formed another relationship outside of ours. *"Was that love?"* I asked myself. No, it was not love! So, that relationship ended. So many questions went through my mind. What does the world have to offer me? Can it offer me love? Can I find a man in the world who can love me? How naïve I was.

When I reached adulthood, at the age of 21, which is the age I have always considered to be that of an adult, I was introduced to what the world had to offer. Yes, I was interested! I began partying—you could not keep me out of the club. I started doing things out of my character, which was totally contrary to the way I had been raised—drinking, smoking, and simulating (imitate) things I saw other people doing. "Was this me?" I asked. No, no, no! I was still young, confused and broken, and I had a baby. I could not possibly find love in the world.

What I did find was a man whose eyes fell upon me as I walked to my car around 3:00 a.m. as I was leaving the club dressed like I was trying to catch a man. I was wearing shorts that nearly showed my bottom, a halter-top that revealed more of my flesh, and I cannot forget those three-inch heels. After this man had approached me—with those brown eyes and standing about 6 foot 3 tall —he shared that he had noticed me in the club. I was thinking to myself: *"This might be the kind of man I need. He is handsome. He is older. He seems to be mature. You know, he might know how to treat a lady.* The question was, "Was I being a lady?"

Shortly after that night, we started to communicate. I felt the need to share with him the experiences I had in my prior relationships. He seemed to have been very concerned. He listened, although there was more. I had attracted a lying, manipulative, controlling man who only loved my body. I was silly to think he wanted anything more. I found myself in another relationship. About a year later, this relationship ended. I realized he had something in common with the other men I had dated. All of them had a lack of respect for women. After this relationship came to a close, I asked myself, *"When am I going to meet the right man?"*

I will take you a little further — another relationship — another transition — and another child brought into this brokenness that was still within me. At the age of 23, I gave birth to my second child. This was a different father, but similar characteristics. This was very challenging for me because I did not want to fit in this group of having baby after baby with different fathers. I grew up in a house with 12 siblings, with the same father, so this was very hard for me. Besides, I wanted to be married with my second child, but this could not happen because I did not want to marry anyone who had the characteristics of my father.

I was young with two babies. Nonetheless, I was in transition again. I had even met the father of my second child in the club. He seemed very nice, but he represented that part of my father that was very good at describing women as female dogs. So this relationship ended after three years of often being labeled as a "female dog." I know you are probably asking yourself, "What was she thinking?" Well, the truth is, I was not thinking. I was searching in all the wrong places, looking for what only God could give. It was also nothing new to be called a "female dog." I had heard this since I was a child—so that was the "norm."

I was thankful for my second child, but I realized I chose the route of partying instead of continuing my education. Continuing my education would have closed not only the learning gaps that existed between the ages of 17 and 23 (as I later realized in pursuing my bachelor's degree), but would have helped me to focus my attention more positively. I am not saying that going to college would have prevented me from having another child, but I do believe that my focus would have been more in harmony with overall progress. By this I mean the principles instilled in me as a child concerning education would have been more likely thought upon if that choice had been made. But like most young folk, I wanted to at least try this thing they called, "partying."

After partying for years, long enough to have received my bachelor's degree, I was going nowhere and made a high-impact decision to simply shift my focus—change my life. I was partying and seeking love from those who did not know love themselves, so they could not possibly offer it. I wanted to escape the hurt by having fun, which consisted of drinking and an occasional smoke of "natural herb," all of which had taken a toll on me. Not long after this, I found myself drunk on hopes and dreams of making a better life for my family and high off all the possibilities of achieving my goals.

At this point, my heart, mind, and soul where united in truth. The truth was I was not living life as the person and mother I was purposed to be. So, I decided to go to college, and I started in August 1998. I went full-time for years until I received my bachelor's degree in 2002. As a single mother, I knew I wanted to offer my children more than a lifestyle of partying every weekend. But one thing I struggled with was being with a man. I felt as though I needed a man. These transitions continued.

At the age of 26, I got married for the first time. I thought he was the love of my life. He was financially stable, a provider and good looking. Sounds a bit like my father, huh? You could not tell me anything. I was affectionate, intimate, and I cooked, cleaned, washed his clothes, ironed his work uniforms, delivered his lunch, took care of the children, prayed over the family, and much more. In essence, I was being my mother. That is, loving, caring, giving, and recognizing the importance of submitting to my mate. In reality, I was denied the experience of true love. I gave so much love, but I did not receive the same love in return.

Let me tell you though, I nagged, fussed, and complained. Now that was not healthy at all. I was an angry woman. I had to have the last word. In Proverbs 21:19 we read, "It's better to dwell in the wilderness, than with a contentious and angry woman." Well, that is just what he started doing — coming home late, cheating, and not spending quality time with the family.

I realized that I shared some of the characteristics of my father, too. The fussing and anger that I was used to seeing had spilled over into my relationships and marriage. I was still bruised on the inside from my childhood. The marriage had started to fade. My husband and I both contributed to the diminishing of our marriage. We both had our share of issues we had to battle and deal with. The complaining, nagging and fussing just did not go with the lack of spending quality time and cheating. Circumstances forced us to separate in September 2001.

Six months later, I found myself opening up to another relationship — broken and confused. There I was, in transition again. Not only that, I was not even divorced yet from the existing marriage. What was important to me at that time was just having a friendship. I wanted someone to spend quality time with, but I saw someone who was very appealing to my natural eyes. He was tall and handsome. Financially stable? Well, after the experience with my husband, it just did not matter. That is what brokenness and accepting without setting godly standards will do for you.

Was he a provider? Yes, he was a provider, but not as my father and other men in my relationships had been. He, this prince charming, provided something uniquely different. He could have a decent conversation covering a broad range of subjects, laugh and joke. God seemed to be one of our favorite topics. Did I consult God about this friendship? Not right off. Did I think about my children? No. Well, that should have been the most important concern, but I was absolutely selfish. I admit that.

Can a man be in your life and not in your children's life? Yes, this is possible. Was the inner man or spirituality important to me? Yes, and since then I have come to know that conversation is one thing, faith — practicing what we preach — is another. A person knows a tree by the fruit it bears, right? Could I have lived by myself? Yes. Would I advise women to ultimately wait on God? Yes. I have now learned that it is important to fall in love with Him in your singleness. Read on!

After a year and a half of dating this man, I was saying, "I do" for the second time. I reluctantly (to hesitate) said "I do!" I did it anyway although I was clearly warned and convinced that this was not the man for me. Okay, I was disobedient. You know sometimes you just have to learn the hard way, as my mother would say. I heard that statement so many times growing up. You may have heard your parents say the same thing as my parents said.

You see, that marriage was built on adultery—lies, deceit, and lust. Although I thought of all the wonderful things I could do to make my marriage work, I failed to realize this marriage simply would not work because it was not put together by God. The seed of disobedience had been sown and I was reaping the harvest.

Prior to, and during the marriage, God dealt with me on the seeds that had been sown after separation during my first marriage. There was no peace or joy in my spirit. I began to hear sermons on adultery and being unequally yoked. Unequally yoked means that two people are not on one accord with God; so maybe the husband is saved and the wife is not, or maybe the wife is saved and the husband is not. The heated arguments in this marriage led to my having frequent migraine headaches. I was taking an excessive amount of aspirin to relieve the pain which left me with skin bruises, major hair loss, and an endoscope surgery to locate any ulcers—all due to taking aspirins extensively because of a house divided against itself.

He and I finally separated. My children and I were left living in a house with no gas, which we needed for seven months for heat to stay warm and for cooking. I was drained spiritually, emotionally, mentally, socially, financially, and physically at that point. I was broken, but I was still standing! And I am "STILL STANDING" after so many years later! I knew only God could restore me.

I was one who worried about what other people had to say. I did not want to feel the shame and guilt of my decision. We often make choices, but we fail to realize all of these choices come with a consequence. The Word of God tells us to choose life or death. Choosing life can bring forth many blessings from God. On the other hand, choosing death can bring forth many curses. (Deuteronomy 30:19). It seems as though I was choosing all the negatives when it came to my life.

In February 2004, pending a divorce, I was living a single life again, with my two children. I was still a little vulnerable, but I was committed to recovery. I was headed toward the road to healing and deliverance! I had to tell myself no more going from man to man. I had the time to self-examine and evaluate the life I was living and my actions as a result of my thinking. Living a life for God and being a good role model for my children was my first priority. A path of freedom, righteousness, peace, and truth was standing before me – and this is the course I wanted to take!

PART THREE

I was 12 years old when I first learned of Jesus and His purpose. Well, I guess I should say I was 12 years old when I gained a clearer understanding of who He is. My father would tell us that Jesus had so much power. As I started reading the Bible for myself, I learned that His power was true. Jesus was sent to earth so that He could direct us back to our Heavenly Father. I read about how He healed the broken-hearted, set the captives free, cast out devils, and performed many other miracles. He was the One who took the keys from hell.

Our family would have Bible study in our living room at least once a week, with the exception of those times my father would order my mother to wake us up at 3:00 a.m. or 4:00 a.m. to read the Bible to us. He would share many stories in the Bible of those who had been used by God before Jesus ever walked the earth. He would share the stories of Abraham, Isaac and Jacob. He told us that God is the reason we live, breathe, walk and talk. But one thing my father did in the process of us having those early morning Bible sessions was—cuss at us, while holding the Bible in his hands. I know you are saying, "You have got to be kidding, Ms. Yolanda." But, no, I am not kidding! This is real.

My father would call one of our names and ask, "What did I just read?" If we could not repeat the Scripture he had read, we were going to get a whipping. Yes, even if we were too sleepy to focus — well, that included all of us because all of us were too tired at that time of the morning. Mind you, we still had to go to school, after being awakened so early. (*I once said to myself, now how can a man that could expound on the Word of God as he did be so controlling...and cuss with the Bible in his hands?*).

Because of my father's aggressive, dominating approach in teaching us about the Bible, there was a certain fear planted within me that made it difficult for me to even want to even read the Bible. My siblings also felt the same. Since I had been an adult and blessed with a deeper understanding of the Bible, I am not only thankful God for His miracle-working power, but for the greatest power of all: The power to forgive, nurture, correct and protect. I thank Him for health and strength, and for certain gifts and talents He has placed on the inside of me and others — even for the small things that are the big things some people forget about or take for granted.

I was taught to pray every night. Even before I accepted God, I prayed. I would say to myself, "If anybody can create me, then I know they've got me." But as a child I did not know I really had to accept Him. I questioned, "Why anybody wouldn't want to accept Him?" At one point, it was hard for me to accept Him.

I got saved (accepted Jesus as my Lord and Savior) at the age of 25 and that is when I made the choice to follow Him. I still had faults, and had not yet tasted wholeness, but I learned that He had a plan and purpose for my life. I was created by Him to fulfill my destiny. I joined First Baptist Church, Acipco, under the leadership of the late Pastor Vincent Provitt. I started singing in the choir and serving God. This was a big shift for me, yet a roadmap to my ultimate purpose. I was a baby Christian, but I knew that God wanted to do something awesome in my life that was waiting to be birthed out of me in a season such as now.

Later, I joined Full Gospel Fellowship Church, under the leadership of Pastor Willie L. Brown, Jr. This church was truly geared toward helping to restore those who had been abused on some level. He definitely shared the uncompromising Word of God—he was straight to the point. You were not going to hear a watered down sermon, nor one that made you feel good. Also, he had a way of challenging his members to go to the level that God has for us all. I served as a worship leader and youth praise dance leader for a short time. I was also on the prayer warrior team and I was part of our women's ministry. This was an area of ministry that God tested and developed in me. I had the opportunity to minister to a group of women at our 2005 Annual Women's Conference. Prior to that, I was chosen to share a "Word" during the pastor's anniversary the same year, and then another opportunity prior to that. It felt good to be a part of God's family and to share his Word with others through the different church ministries I was involved in.

In the midst of all this, God had revealed to my former pastor that ministry was definitely in me. It was in 2007 when my purpose was shared through a profound thought—and that still small voice had spoken to me. The small voice shared with me that my purpose is to minister to women through my writing. I am very thankful for a new beginning and a new level!

The Bible makes more sense to me now that I have matured spiritually. I am not only looking at things through my natural eyes but also my spiritual eyes. The life of Jesus was so awesome. Yes, He performed so many miracles. Once I read the Gospels (maybe you have heard your pastor teach out of the Bible the book of Mark, Luke, John and Matthew), I learned that He spoke many parables. Even though His disciples walked with Him daily, He could only reveal things to them based on their level of maturity. It is the same way now. As I reflect on my childhood, I can see clearly that learning of Him created a desire in me to now do as Jesus did.

Just like I heard of Jesus, I would hear stories of an enemy — the kind of enemy that is common to all of us — and that is Satan. You know the one who causes the chaos and brings many adverse circumstances in our lives. Yes, he does. You may have heard of him being called the devil, an adversary and the prince of the air. Satan is just the plan old evil one.

When I was a child I would often be attacked by spirits, but I did not know why. I would question my mother and father about the many attacks that I was experiencing, being so young. Literally, there would be times that I could not even move my body. As I grew older, I would hear stories of how Satan knows your purpose before you ever thought about it, and he came to steal, kill and destroy our lives. I have learned that our life here on earth is all about purpose. It is about knowing and fulfilling our purpose whether we realize that or not. I have also learned that Satan will do whatever he can to take control of your mind and hinder you from fulfilling your ultimate purpose.

Speaking of purpose, it was my purpose that the enemy started attacking when I was young, like some of you, trying to block what God has intended. The things I said I would never subject myself to are the exact things the enemy played on—and has always played on. It seems as though he scoped me out as a child, maybe you, too. Okay, let me put it in another way. Sadly, the very things I observed as a child, which was contrary to God's purpose in and for the family, were those very things that the devil tried to use to keep me in prison in my mind.

You may ask yourself what I mean by this. Well, the things I thought would happened to me and what I feared most did happen. I found myself losing everything I had as a result of my thinking and speaking, which led to bad relationship choices, along with my overall brokenness.

I was scarred as a child. And the broken child that once lived in me for many, many years has just recently been healed through confession, meditation, prayer, seeking, faith and love. I was a child that missed some of the important things that I needed to be an effective, healthy-minded and well-balanced adult, especially concerning dating.

As I observed my parents' marriage, I thought relationships should be based on how their relationship was. I wanted to prevent having someone like my father, but I found myself attracting men who were in essence like my father. They were broken too. I have come to know that it is not uncommon to live by what you observe as a child. It is rather easy to accept the things that are unacceptable, because in your little innocent mind you think it is all right. I grew determined not to give the enemy any place in my life.

Before I end my story, I want to share with you how I was delivered me from the very thing that had me bound for a long time (transitioning from man to man). And the weakness I had been yielding to is what God used to bring deliverance — and that is a man.

One day, I met a minister, who happens to be my dear friend. I opened up the line of communication with him. He said that God gave him a vision that a woman would come into his life and that his purpose was for us to help each other to get to the next level. Shortly after having that vision, he said that he was led to the church I was a member of, and he knew at a youth ministry meeting that I was that young lady, because God had shown him. He said that it was something about the presence in the room. At first, I did not initially connect with the reasons for him coming into my life, but as time progressed, I began to see the scope of it.

After communicating with him for the first time, he was able to identify with my brokenness. He stated, "God wants to deliver you from people, and I can tell that you have been emotionally wounded." I was amazed that he knew that, even before I shared my story. That is the kind of God we serve. You see, He knows who, when, why and how to deliver you from anything or anyone that is not good for you. Again, it was not easy to accept the reasons for him coming into my life. Why? Because coming out of many transitions, this was a comfort zone. So my thoughts of him being the one for me is what was running through my mind. But God actually used him to help me to grow spiritually. I can even remember him saying, in the first stages of our friendship, "Yo, growing pains don't always feel good."

I must admit, I was still struggling with being patient—I was a "right now" woman. You see, relationship dependency was the "norm." But I needed to practice patience and wait on God to move in every part of my life, even concerning a mate.

I could feel the change that was about take place in my life. Something new was about to happen. I had become aware of all the things that had been holding me back, the mistakes I had made, and the bad relationships that I had gone through. God began to heal me from all the hurt and pain of my childhood and early adulthood. I began to read more and more truth-based books. There were many books that helped me, such as, *Why? Because You Are Anointed* written by T.D. Jakes! *8 Ways to Overcome Adversity* written by Joyce Meyer! *Seduction Exposed* written by Dr. Greenwald! *Expect the Extraordinary* written by Jerry Savella! *My Spiritual Inheritance* written by Juanita Bynum! I began thinking in the direction God was trying to take me. I can truly say all of these books and more helped me to gain the knowledge and understanding I was craving. This was really important because I knew that I needed both of them, along with wisdom to make better decisions.

I was determined not to get involved in another relationship until God was ready to unite me with "***the man***" He desires for me — for the purpose of marriage and ministry. Falling in love with God was all I needed. I began to see that it was more about my relationship with Him than anything else. Since then, I have been able to experience all of His goodness and glory. I can say that I was set free from the agony of unfruitful relationships. It was only because of His grace and mercy that I did not lose my mind. You see, I basically had my own agenda. I was a broken vessel, searching for love. I am now convinced that if I just wait on God, everything will be all right, and God will bless me in every aspect of my life.

ONE
A ROADMAP TO VIRTUE...CRACKING THE SHELL TO BREAK THE YOLK

IFyour parents were planning to take a family trip, where would you want to go? Some of you might say Disney World, White Waters, or Six Flags over Georgia, just to name a few. Your parents may use a roadmap to get to these places if they plan to drive their vehicle. Here is an illustration I would like to show you that requires a roadmap, which is used to help get people from one destination to the next. With this example, we will say that your parents decided to go to Disney World in Florida. Mind you, I am trying to go somewhere with this illustration.

Some of your parents will have shorter routes, and some will have longer routes. Since there are different routes, some of them may come to bumpy roads, dead end streets, have multiple hills to pull, and so on. But they will all get to their destination if the directions are followed as given on the roadmap. When they finally arrive at their destination, they will see how valuable (and important) the roadmap really is.

Some of them may turn around because the road trip seems to long, and some may decide not to go at all. Now that is not to say that those who turn around and stop midways will not eventually get there. They might just need some encouragement along the way. Those who decide not to go will need an extra push.

The conclusion of this illustration is that God works just the same as a roadmap. He, in essence, is the roadmap. He wants to guide you little girls from one destination to the next—take you from level to level— even higher than you can think about. Many of you might get off course, lose focus, but you will all arrive there someday.

You see, you all started out when you were conceived in your mother's womb. What I mean by this is that when your mother was pregnant, it was you that was on the inside of her; meaning you was already a life that was waiting to be delivered into this world. You were all birthed with a purpose. You all have a destiny to fulfill. You will face difficult things in life. More importantly, you were all born with the seed of virtue. What I mean by virtue is basically that you can always do what is right and be seen as a good, little girl. You are all God's daughters, and He loves you so much, more than you will ever know.

There is something that I would like to share though— many of you are broken. To help you understand what I mean by broken, I would like to share this analogy: If you were to pour water in a glass and it shatters as you pick it up off the table, then your water will spill, right? Once that glass shatters it can no longer be used for what it should be used for—and that is to drink liquid {water, juice, or soda} from. We as humans are the same way—if we are shattered (broken), how can we be effective? I want you to understand that people can be broken in many areas of their lives. This would include mentally, emotionally, socially, or spiritually.

Out of the millions upon millions of girls in the world, there are a lot of them who are broken. The brokenness that you may be experiencing could be as a result of something bad that may have happened to you. Whether it was your father, mother, brother, sister, extended relative, even a stranger who hurt or confused you—it has had a negative impact on your life. You must become whole, and I want to assure you that you can become whole with God's help. I will talk about wholeness later in this book.

It is a blessing that your mother, father, aunt, grandmother or some other positive figure in your life thought enough of you to select this book for you to read—a valuable book that will help you as you grow.

TWO
I HURT SOMETIMES

THEREare so many of you girls who are wearing hurt "all over your face." Some people can easily detect that something is wrong with you when they look at you. Many of you show signs of discomfort, anger, and sadness...HURT.

Many of you are hurting within because of something that has happened to you, and some of you are hurting because of what you are now facing in your life. You may have friends that "smile in your face," yet they talk about you behind your back, and some may even steal from you. You may have an absent parent that keeps lying to you. You may live in a home with parents that fuss and fight all the time. There could be a number of things that's contributing to the hurt that you feel.

Are you ready to release (let go) the hurt that you are feeling? I hope that your answer is "Yes." If so, I want you to know that you can release the hurt to your Heavenly Father (God). His Word says, "Come unto me, all ye that labour and are heavy laden (hurt, confused, worried...), and I will give you rest. Take my yoke upon you, and learn of me, for I am meek and lowly in heart: and ye shall find rest unto your souls" (Read Matthew

11:28-29). As you read these scriptures, you will gain the strength to release any and everything to God.

Sometimes when you feel hurt, it does not immediately go away, but the more you talk to God, the less hurt you will feel. Remember, He will comfort you 24 hours a day.

THREE
CRYING WHEN NO ONE IS AROUND

SOME of you girls may be dealing with so many things. Sometimes you just want to get from around everyone and cry. You may be wondering if anyone hears your cry. You may have a good reason to cry; however, some of you may feel that crying will fix everything that is going on in your life. While crying offers a temporary relief, there is a great need to get to the root of your problem. What is causing you to be sad, discouraged, or troubled? I have shared this several times in this book: you must talk to someone you can trust.

I want you to understand that there are some bad things that can happen in life that can have the best of us (children and adults) feeling low. Most of our thinking will be consumed on whatever (lack of money, homelessness, sickness, parents divorcing, etc.) is causing sadness in our lives.

When you girls allow yourselves to stay in the "sad zone," you will not focus on the good things in life. I have good news. The Bible says, "…weeping may endure for a night, but joy cometh in the morning" (Read Psalm 30:5). If you meditate on this scripture everyday (I literally mean every single day), you will learn that joy will transcend {rise above} everything that is causing you to "cry your eyes out."

FOUR
VISUALIZING WHO YOU ARE

IT is important that you answer the following questions so that you can visualize (form a mental image of) who you are. The answers to these questions determine whether or not you see yourself in a negative or positive way.

- Do you feel that you are pretty?
- Do you feel that you are not pretty?
- Is it possible you may have low self-esteem? If so, where does that come from?
- Have you experienced something bad as a child?
- Do your peers talk about you at school? Do they call you ugly? Do they call you fat? Do they call you nasty?
- Have you been told that you are not going to make it far in life?
- Has anyone touched you in the wrong way?
- Did all this leave you broken?

I want you to understand that you are beautiful and smart—full of talent and gifts, no matter who says you are not. God saw fit to create you from the supernatural work of His spiritual hands. He shaped and formed you perfectly. In His creating you, He knew exactly what He was doing. That means you are definitely not a mistake. You possess so much, but because of the negative things people have told you, you have struggled with the acceptance of who you really are.

When a negative image of yourself have been planted in your mind, the tendency to attract negative things in your life will be great—the law of attraction is now in full effect. Your drive to move forward is not even there after the negative images have been planted. If you think about all the negative things that have been said or have happened to you up to this point in your life, it will discourage you from doing things that you desire to do. Some of you want to sing. Some of you want to write books. Some of you want to play an instrument. Some of you want to cheer in school. Some of you want to play sports. You have to see yourself doing the things you really want to do.

It is necessary to change the way you visualize yourself. Your actions are driven by what you see, and what you see is driven by what you think. You see, to start you will **think** about the negative or positive, then you begin to **see** whatever that something is, then you paint a mental picture, if you will, and then you **act**. Did you get that? Here are the ingredients. **Think**. **Visualize**.

Act. I encourage you to always think positive no matter what.

I want to share with you girls that I was a woman who did not feel beautiful on the outside because my self-esteem had been attacked as a child. I was completely broken. I bore the hurt of what I was told as a child, and even what happened to me as a child. I carried that through my teens and into my early adulthood, but when I was made whole—totally delivered from people—I learned to accept everything about me.

I want to let you little girls know that once you are healed on the inside, the light of God will shine bright in your life and draw people to a wonderful, beautiful, anointed, spirit-filled girl. As you grow, you will realize that you are only a tool used by God (I will share more about this later), and you will begin to care less of what people think and say about you and more of who He has made and declared you to be. To add to this, you can start replacing all the negative images with positive ones. When you do that, you will see a major difference in your life.

FIVE
YOU ARE PRETTY ENOUGH

WHEN you look in the mirror every morning you wake up, you should say, "I am pretty enough. I am a beautiful Gem and God loves me. He didn't make any mistakes on me." You have to come to a place in your life where you can honestly say that; knowing that you are pretty whether someone tells you or not or whether you get your nails polished or not or whether you get your hair styled a certain way or not or whether you wear lip gloss or not.

Many of you are depending on someone to tell you that you are pretty; therefore, you find it hard to tell yourself. Some of you feel that you are not pretty enough unless you wear new clothes and lip gloss. Some of you may feel that you are not pretty when you don't get your nails polished. Some of you may feel that you are not pretty because you don't have the latest, brand-named shoes, clothes, etc. Remember, these are material things, and your beauty can never be defined by them.

If someone ever makes you feel that you are required to have a lot of material things (clothes, shoes, jewelry, etc.) to have the "pretty girl status," you need to know that this is untrue. You have to know in your heart, mind, spirit, and soul that you are "pretty enough" because God says you are. You (yes, you little girl) were perfectly made in His image, and everything about our God is beautiful.

SIX
YOU ARE IMPORTANT

MANYof you little girls feel that you are not important; that you don't mean anything to anyone; that your life does not matter. I have good news: you are important to your family, your true friends, and most importantly, you are a very, special jewel to God.

Some of you may have experienced abandonment (to be given up, left alone), lack of love, lack of support, etc. All these things can make you feel least important. You may have even had someone to tell you that you were not important. They may have told you that you are sorry, no good, stupid, and that you would never be anything in life.

I want to encourage you to be careful not to let what someone says to you discourage you because negative words can make you mad, sad or confused. You need to release it right away and learn how to protect {to cover} your ears. You have to determine whether or not you are going to entertain {to hold in mind} what you hear.

You must practice ignoring anything that a person says to you that will make you feel like you are not important. You must also ignore words that are used to attack your character (the quality that makes a person) or your existence.

SEVEN
YOU CAN SHINE LIKE A DIAMOND

YOU are God's little daughter and you are just like a diamond. You may be thinking, "What is a diamond?" A diamond is "a precious stone consisting of a clear and typically colorless crystalline form of pure carbon, the hardest naturally occurring substance." It is a very valuable piece of stone. A diamond ring is even made with this piece of stone.

The reflection of a diamond ring can be seen from afar. It shines with a sparkling glow. That is amazing, isn't it? I want you to know that God will make sure you shine just like a diamond ring. This is to say, as a diamond can be seen among common rocks, you also will shine as a diamond among your family, community, at school—everywhere you go.

You are valuable just like a diamond, too. As you grow, I want you to always remember that. I don't want you to ever think that you are not valued. You are cherished, valued and loved by your family and so many other people. Most importantly, you mean the absolute world to God. He loves you more than you could ever imagine. He is the One who created you to shine like a diamond. I want you to say this, "I will shine like a diamond every day of my life."

EIGHT
YOU CAN LEARN HOW TO LOVE YOURSELF

WHEN you learn how to love yourself, you will accept every part of you. You can and will have a great measure of self-respect, self-confidence, and a high self-esteem. You must understand though if you have low self-esteem, which is one of the most common barriers (something that blocks, prevents) to loving yourself, it may be kind of hard for you; however, it can be corrected. Let me tell you how: you must tell yourself daily that you will love yourself no matter what. As a matter of fact, I want you to point to yourself now and say, "I love me."

There are many of you who may find that hard to do, but this is something that you must do. You have to speak to your heart, emotions (your feelings), and mind – your entire being; knowing that you can love who you are, even as a little girl.

When you learn how to love yourself, you will not easily accept bad behavior nor execute (carry out) bad behavior. You will know what it means to have morals. What I mean by this is that you will be concerned about your reputation, image, and character; ensuring that you are carrying yourself in a godly manner every day.

NINE
YOU CAN HAVE SELF-RESPECT

YOU should focus on respecting yourself every day. You must understand that you cannot disrespect yourself and expect to be respected by other people. It does not happen this way. There are many ways girls disrespect themselves: dressing in an inappropriate way, using bad language, are just to name a few.

I want to give you two examples to help you understand the difference between a girl who respects herself verses a girl who disrespects herself. After I share these examples, I want you to determine which girl you think appears to have no self-respect.

Example 1: A girl gets out of the car to go into the grocery store. She is wearing a mini-skirt that is right below her bottom and a shirt that is revealing her stomach. As she approaches the store, she meets a group of boys who is coming out of the store and notices how she is dressed. One of the boys says something inappropriately to her, and then he asks for her phone number. She tells him to hold on, and she bends over and everyone can see her bottom (rear end) and then she walks over and gives him her number and whispers in his ear, "Call me anytime."

Example 2: A girl is walking down the hall at school, and she passes a group of boys who are contemplating skipping class. She is wearing a t-shirt and denim jeans that are loosely fit. One of the boys says something inappropriately to her, and then asks for her phone number. She politely says, "No thank you, I am not interested. She then proceeds to walk in her class.

Which one is an example of a girl who appears to have no self-respect? What do you think she can do to change her behavior? Do you think that she is seeking attention? Could it be possible that she has low self-esteem?

As you grow little girls, I don't ever want you to carry yourself in the manner the girl in example 1 did. She was seeking attention from the opposite sex. Some girls seek attention for various reasons. A father may not be in the home or there may be a father present in the home, but he is abusive toward the mother (and his children), and a combination of other things. Some girls may be raised by a single mother who has no time for her children. All of these things could possibly lead to "attention seeking" from other sources.

What I have learned over the years is that many girls (and women) desperately seek attention from those of the opposite sex. Sometimes when a person is seeking validation (approval) from a male (boy or man), they will do all manners of degrading things, and dressing inappropriately is just one of them. In order not to carry out this kind of behavior, it is very important that you love who you are so that you won't ever feel the need to be validated by anyone of the opposite sex. To be perfectly honest, you need to let God validate you. Your parents should validate you, too. They need to tell you great things about yourself and encourage you to respect yourself in and out of their presence.

TEN
YOU CAN HAVE HEALTHY EMOTIONS

YOURemotions (the way you feel)can sometimes be good or bad, unhealthy or healthy. What I want you girls to learn as you grow is how to have healthy emotions. When a person is broken (refer to the analogy I shared earlier), they will often experience unhealthy emotions. And when a person experiences unhealthy emotions, they will most likely think negatively.

When someone thinks in a negative manner, their emotions will lead to bad decision-making. I will give you an example to help you understand what I mean by this. Here is an example: a little girl decides to slap another little girl because she thinks the girl said something bad about her. This example shows the girl who slapped the other girl made a poor decision based on what she was thinking. I want to point out that so many of you have let your negative emotions lead you into harmful things as describe in the example.

You must learn to grab a hold of your emotions while you are young, ensuring that you are feeding your mind with things that will make you think healthy. You should think about what you want to be in life, how you plan to achieve your goals, what college you plan to attend, etc. Positive thoughts will attract positive results to result in your favor — in every area of your life. Therefore, you can have healthy emotions.

ELEVEN
YOU CAN HAVE A HEALTHY SELF-ESTEEM

IT is so important for you little girls to have a healthy self-esteem. Having a healthy self-esteem will help build the confidence needed in order to accomplish great things in life. Go ahead and smile and start feeling good about yourself and expect great things to happen for you! When you have a healthy self-esteem, it, too, leads to positive, healthy thinking.

I want to share that you will feel a sense of independence (not under the control of) when you have a healthy self-esteem. You will never feel like you need someone to tell you that you are pretty, you are smart, you are important, you are talented, and so forth. Although these things are good to hear, it will not easily affect you if someone does not tell you.

However, if you are a little girl who has low self-esteem, you probably see yourself as a "nobody," and you do not feel like you are worthy. Some of you feel that your life does not even matter. Wait a minute—it does matter. I want you to start learning how to appreciate who you are, value who you are, and love who you are. Going forward, you should start seeing yourself through the eyes of God. What I mean by this is that you can ask

God to help you see yourself as He sees you. Once you do this, you will only see a beautiful, little girl.

TWELVE
YOU CAN HAVE A POSITIVE ATTITUDE

IT can be very hard for you when you do not have a positive attitude. As you grow, you may hear someone say that "attitude determines your altitude, "if you haven't already heard it. What this basically means is that your attitude determines how far you will go in life. When you have a positive attitude blessings and favor will manifest (be made real) in your life! You will receive gifts, compliments, money, and a number of things, even when you are not expecting it—all because of your positive attitude. Can you remember those times your parents rewarded you when they told you to do something around the house and you did not have a frown on your face nor did you talk back? You may have wanted new clothes, shoes, money, or something else, and you received it all because of your positive attitude.

You must understand that people feel good about a person when they have a positive attitude. They like the positive energy that is released from that person being around them. Likewise, people will not want to be around you when your attitude is bad. It may be a challenge (special effort) for you to receive help from people when your attitude is not pleasant, too. I am certain that you want good things to happen for you, and you want to always do some great things in life; therefore, you have to let God fill your heart with love so that the attitude problem that some of you may have as a little girl can be erased.

If you are a girl who feels that you do not have a positive attitude because of something bad that you have gone through or now facing in your life, I want to encourage you to ask God to help you and not to let that "something" cause you to have a bad attitude. As a matter of fact, you can ask God to fix your attitude. Trust me. He will do it for you.

THIRTEEN
YOU DON'T HAVE TO BE ANGRY

ITis never okay to be angry. Are you an angry, little girl? If so, think about what has caused you to be so angry. Do you believe that people want to be around you when you are angry? Do you like being around angry people?

When you hold anger on the inside of you, it can produce bitterness, hatred, and so many other negative things. When you are angry it can also stop your personal and spiritual growth. What I mean by this is that we as human beings supposed to not only grow physically, but we are supposed to grow in others areas of our lives, too.

I want to let you girls know that it is okay to release the anger. You must first forgive (to stop feeling angry...) anyone that has made you feel this way. When you do this, you can laugh more, love more, and pray more. You will soon find that your anger problem will go away.

In order to be a productive person, you don't want to continue being angry with people. You have to realize that some of the people who you may be angry with is actually happy with their lives. When a person is angry, they freely invite misery into their life. Is this you? If so, you can get free in your mind, spirit and soul. Release the anger so that you can move forward. There are great things ahead of you. Are you ready to experience those great things? I hope that your answer is "Yes."

FOURTEEN
YOU CAN LEARN HOW TO FORGIVE

ITis okay to forgive anyone who has wronged you. What I mean by this is that if someone has said or done something to hurt you, you must learn to forgive them if they say they apologize or if they don't say it. I want you to know that if you don't forgive a person, you will think about what they did over and over again, and you may get upset about it. Do you get upset about what someone has done to you or said to you? If so, what you are actually doing is letting the anger get the best of you.

It is time to forgive. You can learn how to forgive by praying to God, asking for His help. You can call out the person by name that may have hurt you. Ask God to forgive you and forgive them.

I am certain as a little girl you have not been offended a lot of times, but as you grow you may find that you will probably be offended by other people numerous times. The most important thing to remember is to forgive people every time they offend you. Don't allow yourself to become so mad to where you cannot say, "I am sorry if you offend someone," and accept someone's apology (and forgive) if they say, "I am sorry for what I said or did to you. Will you forgive me?"

FIFTEEN
YOU CAN LEARN HOW TO PRAY

PRAYERis when someone talks to God and He talks back to them. That means you can share your thoughts, pains, joys, and anything else by opening your mouth and speaking to God. Prayer is important, necessary, and it is very much needed in order to have a healthy relationship with Him. I want you to know that this is the greatest relationship you can ever have.

Some of you have already learned to communicate with God by simply praying, "Thou lay me down to sleep, I pray to the Lord my soul to keep, if I should die before I wake, I pray to the Lord my soul to take." I prayed that prayer when I was a little girl. Do you know that your relationship with Him will grow even more as you pray more? While praying you can ask God to lead you every day, to take care of your family, to bless you to make good grades in school, to bless your parents, to bless your teachers and to bless everyone else, too.

Prayer will allow you to be open in telling Him about anything. Just imagine talking to your earthly father about something that's been bothering you, whether it is about a friend, a personal matter, or even about a bad experience that you had at school. If he loves you, he is going to offer support and comfort to help you get through it. Now I want you to know that God loves you even more. He will comfort you when you are not feeling well. He will make sure you have everything you need from food to clothing to shelter and so much more.

It is important for you learn how to pray so that you can make it through some difficult times in your life. You are little now, but as you grow, you will face some things in life and that is when you will learn to appreciate what it means to pray. I want you to know that you cannot always depend on someone else's prayers. What I mean by this is that your mother, father, pastor, teacher or some other adult may pray for and with you now. And I am certain these people will always keep you in their prayers. But there are times when you are going to have to pray to God for yourself. You will always need God in your life, and you need to always pray about every thing. If you are thinking, "everything," yes, I mean every little thing in life.

SIXTEEN
WHOLENESS IS FOR LITTLE GIRLS TOO

YOU can experience wholeness as a little girl. To help you to understand what I mean by wholeness, I want you to go back and read the analogy that I gave at the beginning of the book to help you to understand what I mean by brokenness. After reading this analogy again, just imagine that glass that I describe not being shattered; meaning it can be used for its' original purpose, and that is to hold liquid (water, juice soda) for you to drink.

As I shared before, many little girls (teen girls and women) are broken, just as a "shattered" glass. If you are broken you must realize that you do not have to carry this brokenness into your teenage and adulthood. Wholeness is available to all of God's children. When a person becomes whole, it allows them to be all that God has purposed them to be. For example, your pastor at church has been purposed be a preacher; meaning she or he can teach the Word of God to help people to do the right thing in life and to grow spiritually. Another example, your teacher's purpose is to teach you so that you can become a great citizen as an adult and accomplish great things in life. Therefore, just as the drinking glass is used for a certain purpose, God has created you to be used for a certain purpose as those in the examples that I shared.

There is also a certain level of peace that comes with wholeness. When you are peaceful, it releases positive energy into the atmosphere—in the home, at church, at school—wherever you go. More importantly, wholeness will shed light on that seed of virtue (you) and make it develop.

When any of us (even little girls) are broken the devil will use it to his advantage to keep us in a place of misery. The devil will tell you a lie; that God will not heal your broken heart, erase your pain, or dry your tears, but you have to tell Him boldly that "he is a liar."Having been a person who was once broken and now experiencing wholeness, I remember having that feeling that I would remain the same—that there was no freedom for me and I had to continue living in shame. I realized that I had to let go of the shame and guilt and see myself in light of who God created me to be—a virtuous woman who could live a free life and be an effective being. You will share the same experience if you desire wholeness, and I want you to know that you can experience wholeness as a little girl.

7 DAY PRAYERS AND AFFIRMATIONS

DAY1

Prayer: *Lord, I don't know if I am broken, but if I am, I know that I am healed, delivered, and set free through your great healing powers. I decree that I am made whole. I thank you for giving me that faith to move beyond where I am in my life.*

Affirmation: *I will focus on moving in the direction of healing daily. I will see myself whole, happy, and confident. And this will spill over into my adult life.*

DAY 2

Prayer: *Lord, I thank you for giving me the wisdom and understanding (even as a little girl) of where my brokenness stemmed from. I thank you that I am no longer hidden in the shadow of brokenness. I thank you for giving me the power to break this cycle of brokenness.*

Affirmation: *I choose to live mentally, spiritually, and physically and not die mentally, spiritually, and physically.*

DAY 3

Prayer: *Lord, I thank you that my inner beauty reflects my outer beauty. Lord, I know that I don't need anyone to validate*

95

me — for I am a VIRTUOUS, LITTLE GIRL — filled with your spirit, but help me to accept and appreciate how you created me.

Affirmation: *I am beautiful now, and forever will be. And I have a beautiful heart, and this I know. As a little girl I can do anything I aspire to do because I am smart, intelligent, and gifted.*

DAY 4

Prayer: *Lord, I thank you for giving me your Word as a living principle for my life. I thank you that I can share your Word with my friends, families, and my enemies. I am not too young to learn of you.*

Affirmation: *I will receive your Word daily in my heart so that I can apply it to my life and every situation that present itself to me as a little girl, and even as I grow.*

DAY 5

Prayer: *Lord, I thank you for blessing me to realize how valuable I am to you as a little girl.*

Affirmation: *I demand of myself respect, honor, integrity, and healthy thinking starting now as a little girl.*

DAY 6

Prayer: *Lord, I thank you for giving me wisdom. Lord, help me to use it every day.*

Affirmation: *I will continue to use wisdom throughout the rest of my life.*

DAY 7

Prayer: *Lord, help me to make good decisions daily. I thank you Lord for letting me learn from the bad decisions that I have made as a little girl.*

Affirmation: *I demand of myself a commitment to make good decisions daily.*

FROM VICTIM TO VIRTUOUS FOR LITTLE GIRLS

FROM

VICTIM

TO

VIRTUOUS

for

LIITLE GIRLS

JOURNAL

*

_____

_____

_____

_____

_____

_____

_____

_____

_____

_____

_____

_____

_____

*

_____

_____

_____

_____

_____

_____

_____

_____

_____

_____

_____

_____

_____

*

_____

_____

_____

_____

_____

_____

_____

_____

_____

_____

_____

_____

_____

*

_____

_____

_____

_____

_____

_____

_____

_____

_____

_____

_____

_____

_____

_____

*

_____

_____

_____

_____

_____

_____

_____

_____

_____

_____

_____

_____

_____

*

_____

_____

_____

_____

_____

_____

_____

_____

_____

_____

_____

_____

_____

_____

*

_____

_____

_____

_____

_____

_____

_____

_____

_____

_____

_____

_____

_____

_____

*

_____

_____

_____

_____

_____

_____

_____

_____

_____

_____

_____

_____

_____

_____

*

_____

_____

_____

_____

_____

_____

_____

_____

_____

_____

_____

_____

_____

_____

_____

*

_____

_____

_____

_____

_____

_____

_____

_____

_____

_____

_____

_____

_____

*

_____

_____

_____

_____

_____

_____

_____

_____

_____

_____

_____

_____

_____

_____

*

_____

_____

_____

_____

_____

_____

_____

_____

_____

_____

_____

_____

_____

*

_____

_____

_____

_____

_____

_____

_____

_____

_____

_____

_____

_____

_____

_____

*

_____

_____

_____

_____

_____

_____

_____

_____

_____

_____

_____

_____

_____

*

_____

_____

_____

_____

_____

_____

_____

_____

_____

_____

_____

_____

_____

*

_____

_____

_____

_____

_____

_____

_____

_____

_____

_____

_____

_____

_____

_____

_____

*

_____

_____

_____

_____

_____

_____

_____

_____

_____

_____

_____

_____

_____

*

_____

_____

_____

_____

_____

_____

_____

_____

_____

_____

_____

_____

_____

*

_____

_____

_____

_____

_____

_____

_____

_____

_____

_____

_____

_____

_____

*

_____

_____

_____

_____

_____

_____

_____

_____

_____

_____

_____

_____

_____

_____

*

_____

_____

_____

_____

_____

_____

_____

_____

_____

_____

_____

_____

_____

_____

*

_____

_____

_____

_____

_____

_____

_____

_____

_____

_____

_____

_____

_____

_____

_____

*

_____

_____

_____

_____

_____

_____

_____

_____

_____

_____

_____

_____

_____

_____

_____

*

_____

_____

_____

_____

_____

_____

_____

_____

_____

_____

_____

_____

_____

*

_____

_____

_____

_____

_____

_____

_____

_____

_____

_____

_____

_____

*

_____

_____

_____

_____

_____

_____

_____

_____

_____

_____

_____

_____

_____

_____

_____

*

_____

_____

_____

_____

_____

_____

_____

_____

_____

_____

_____

_____

_____

*

_____

_____

_____

_____

_____

_____

_____

_____

_____

_____

_____

_____

_____

_____

*

_____

_____

_____

_____

_____

_____

_____

_____

_____

_____

_____

_____

_____

*

_____

_____

_____

_____

_____

_____

_____

_____

_____

_____

_____

_____

_____

*

_____

_____

_____

_____

_____

_____

_____

_____

_____

_____

_____

_____

*

_____

_____

_____

_____

_____

_____

_____

_____

_____

_____

_____

_____

_____

*

_____

_____

_____

_____

_____

_____

_____

_____

_____

_____

_____

_____

_____

_____

*

_____

_____

_____

_____

_____

_____

_____

_____

_____

_____

_____

_____

_____

*

_____

_____

_____

_____

_____

_____

_____

_____

_____

_____

_____

_____

_____

*

_____

_____

_____

_____

_____

_____

_____

_____

_____

_____

_____

_____

_____

_____

*

_____

_____

_____

_____

_____

_____

_____

_____

_____

_____

_____

_____

_____

*

_____

_____

_____

_____

_____

_____

_____

_____

_____

_____

_____

_____

_____

_____

*

_____

_____

_____

_____

_____

_____

_____

_____

_____

_____

_____

_____

_____

_____

*

_____

_____

_____

_____

_____

_____

_____

_____

_____

_____

_____

_____

_____

_____

*

_____

_____

_____

_____

_____

_____

_____

_____

_____

_____

_____

_____

_____

*

_____

_____

_____

_____

_____

_____

_____

_____

_____

_____

_____

_____

_____

*

_____

_____

_____

_____

_____

_____

_____

_____

_____

_____

_____

_____

_____

_____

_____

*

_____

_____

_____

_____

_____

_____

_____

_____

_____

_____

_____

_____

_____

*

_____

_____

_____

_____

_____

_____

_____

_____

_____

_____

_____

_____

_____

_____

*

_____

_____

_____

_____

_____

_____

_____

_____

_____

_____

_____

_____

_____

_____

*

_____

_____

_____

_____

_____

_____

_____

_____

_____

_____

_____

_____

_____

_____

*

_____

_____

_____

_____

_____

_____

_____

_____

_____

_____

_____

_____

_____

_____

*

_____

_____

_____

_____

_____

_____

_____

_____

_____

_____

_____

_____

_____

*

_____

_____

_____

_____

_____

_____

_____

_____

_____

_____

_____

_____

_____

_____

*

_____

_____

_____

_____

_____

_____

_____

_____

_____

_____

_____

_____

_____

_____

*

_____

_____

_____

_____

_____

_____

_____

_____

_____

_____

_____

_____

_____

_____

*

_____

_____

_____

_____

_____

_____

_____

_____

_____

_____

_____

_____

_____

*

_____

_____

_____

_____

_____

_____

_____

_____

_____

_____

_____

_____

_____

_____

*

_____

_____

_____

_____

_____

_____

_____

_____

_____

_____

_____

_____

*

_____

_____

_____

_____

_____

_____

_____

_____

_____

_____

_____

_____

_____

_____

_____

_____

*

_____

_____

_____

_____

_____

_____

_____

_____

_____

_____

_____

_____

_____

_____

*

_____

_____

_____

_____

_____

_____

_____

_____

_____

_____

_____

_____

_____

_____

*

_____

_____

_____

_____

_____

_____

_____

_____

_____

_____

_____

_____

_____

*

_____

_____

_____

_____

_____

_____

_____

_____

_____

_____

_____

_____

_____

_____

*

_____

_____

_____

_____

_____

_____

_____

_____

_____

_____

_____

_____

_____

*

_____

_____

_____

_____

_____

_____

_____

_____

_____

_____

_____

_____

_____

*

_____

_____

_____

_____

_____

_____

_____

_____

_____

_____

_____

_____

*

_____

_____

_____

_____

_____

_____

_____

_____

_____

_____

_____

_____

_____

_____

*

_____

_____

_____

_____

_____

_____

_____

_____

_____

_____

_____

_____

_____

_____

*

_____

_____

_____

_____

_____

_____

_____

_____

_____

_____

_____

_____

_____

_____

*

_____

_____

_____

_____

_____

_____

_____

_____

_____

_____

_____

_____

_____

_____

*

_____

_____

_____

_____

_____

_____

_____

_____

_____

_____

_____

_____

_____

_____

*

_____

_____

_____

_____

_____

_____

_____

_____

_____

_____

_____

_____

_____

_____

_____

*

_____

_____

_____

_____

_____

_____

_____

_____

_____

_____

_____

_____

_____

_____

*

_____

_____

_____

_____

_____

_____

_____

_____

_____

_____

_____

_____

_____

_____

*

_____

_____

_____

_____

_____

_____

_____

_____

_____

_____

_____

_____

_____

_____

*

_____

_____

_____

_____

_____

_____

_____

_____

_____

_____

_____

_____

_____

_____

*

_____

_____

_____

_____

_____

_____

_____

_____

_____

_____

_____

_____

_____

_____

*

_____

_____

_____

_____

_____

_____

_____

_____

_____

_____

_____

_____

_____

*

_____

_____

_____

_____

_____

_____

_____

_____

_____

_____

_____

_____

_____

_____

_____

*

_____

_____

_____

_____

_____

_____

_____

_____

_____

_____

_____

_____

_____

_____

*

_____

_____

_____

_____

_____

_____

_____

_____

_____

_____

_____

_____

_____

_____

_____

*

_____

_____

_____

_____

_____

_____

_____

_____

_____

_____

_____

_____

_____

*

_____

_____

_____

_____

_____

_____

_____

_____

_____

_____

_____

_____

_____

_____

*

_____

_____

_____

_____

_____

_____

_____

_____

_____

_____

_____

_____

_____

*

_____

_____

_____

_____

_____

_____

_____

_____

_____

_____

_____

_____

_____

_____

*

_____

_____

_____

_____

_____

_____

_____

_____

_____

_____

_____

_____

_____

_____

*

_____

_____

_____

_____

_____

_____

_____

_____

_____

_____

_____

_____

_____

*

_____

_____

_____

_____

_____

_____

_____

_____

_____

_____

_____

_____

*

_____

_____

_____

_____

_____

_____

_____

_____

_____

_____

_____

_____

_____

*

_____

_____

_____

_____

_____

_____

_____

_____

_____

_____

_____

_____

_____

*

_____

_____

_____

_____

_____

_____

_____

_____

_____

_____

_____

_____

_____

_____

*

_____

_____

_____

_____

_____

_____

_____

_____

_____

_____

_____

_____

*

_____

_____

_____

_____

_____

_____

_____

_____

_____

_____

_____

_____

_____

*

_____

_____

_____

_____

_____

_____

_____

_____

_____

_____

_____

_____

_____

*

_____

_____

_____

_____

_____

_____

_____

_____

_____

_____

_____

_____

*

_____

_____

_____

_____

_____

_____

_____

_____

_____

_____

_____

_____

_____

*

---

*

_____

_____

_____

_____

_____

_____

_____

_____

_____

_____

_____

_____

_____

_____

*

_____

_____

_____

_____

_____

_____

_____

_____

_____

_____

_____

_____

_____

_____

*

_____

_____

_____

_____

_____

_____

_____

_____

_____

_____

_____

_____

_____

*

_____

_____

_____

_____

_____

_____

_____

_____

_____

_____

_____

_____

_____

_____

*

_____

_____

_____

_____

_____

_____

_____

_____

_____

_____

_____

_____

_____

*

_____

_____

_____

_____

_____

_____

_____

_____

_____

_____

_____

_____

_____

_____

_____

*

_____

_____

_____

_____

_____

_____

_____

_____

_____

_____

_____

_____

_____

*

_____

_____

_____

_____

_____

_____

_____

_____

_____

_____

_____

_____

_____

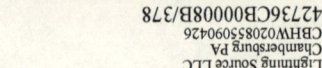